JONAH
POET IN EXTREMIS

RICHARD LITTLEDALE

Richard + Sally,
With my love to
you both.
Strength to you ...

Richard

McKnight
& Bishop
Ltd
Inspire

Scripture quotations taken from the
HOLY BIBLE, NEW INTERNATIONAL VERSION®. NIV® Copyright © 1973, 1978, 1984 by International Bible Society Used by permission of Zondervan. All rights reserved worldwide

ISBN 978-1-905691-20-3
A CIP catalogue record for this book is available from the British Library

First published in 2014 by McKnight & Bishop Inspire, an imprint of

    McKnight & Bishop Ltd.
    28 Grifffiths Court, Bowburn, Co. Durham, DH6 5FD
    http://www.mcknightbishop.com
    info@mcknightbishop .com

This books has been typeset in Garamond and TRAJAN PRO
Printed and bound in Great Britain by Lightning Source Inc, Milton Keynes
The paper used in this book has been made from wood independently certified as having come from sustainable forests.

To all who have found more
when they had less, in extremis.

ABOUT THE AUTHOR

Richard Littledale is the Minister of Teddington Baptist Church, in West London, and has always had an interest in innovative and creative communication.

His book, *Stale Bread*, is a guide to narrative preaching, and the *Preacher's A-Z*, is a preacher's companion on the craft and practice of preaching. His book, *Who Needs Words*, is a comprehensive handbook for Christian communicators.

Richard has been a regular contributor to Pause for Thought on BBC Radio 2 as well as other radio work on Premier Christian Radio and BBC Radio 4. He is a tutor with the College of Preachers, writes a preachers' blog and tweets regularly.

In 2011 he broke a publishing record when his book, *The Littlest Star* was written, illustrated, designed, printed and placed on sale within three weeks in aid of Shooting Star Chase children's hospices. The book has since visited book fairs in three countries and featured on national and regional BBC radio. Another children's book, *The Tale of The Little Owl*, went from concept to publication in 66 days in 2013 in aid of children's cancer charity, Momentum.

Richard loves stories and sees them as a means to circumvent our cynicism and caution before unleashing the transformative power of God's word.

http://richardlittledale.me.uk
@richardlittleda

TABLE OF CONTENTS

INTRODUCTION

18th June 1976, and I find myself filing into the man hall at Little Heath Comprehensive School, together with the other 100 or so in my year group. Under the watchful eye of our tutors, we sit ourselves down, cross-legged, on the dusty parquet flooring for another assembly. Today's at least, will be different – as there is a guest speaker. He is from an organisation of which I have never heard, called the Gideons. The man at the front, who looks like somebody's uncle in his tweed jacket, explains that the Gideons place Bibles in hotels, prisons, and schools. At this point my interest is piqued, as I sense a freebie in the offing. Sure enough, as the assembly finishes, every student is handed a shiny New Testament in a burgundy cover with the golden lamp of the Gideons embossed on it. Inside is the whole New Testament, together with a list of explanatory terms, a suggested reading schedule, a guide on where to find help in different circumstances, and a page on which to record the date it was given. It is right there now, in my spidery twelve-year old handwriting, next to an orange squash stain where a drinks bottle leaked in my school bag. Our avuncular Gideon said that the bible was a free gift, but that in return we were asked at least to read it.

That assembly, and its free gift, began a chain of events which is still rolling today as I sit and type. With no church background, and unsure what to do with this unfamiliar book, I joined a lunchtime Christian Union at the school. The meetings were led by a down-to-earth metalwork teacher who smiled and joked as he talked effortlessly about the Bible, God and faith. When I learnt that he ran a club on Sundays too, at my local Baptist church, I was quick to sign up. The club, known back then as Crusaders, created a wonderful opportunity to learn about life and faith, and to familiarise myself further with the New Testament and its strange older cousin, the Old Testament.

Another year, another floor, as I sat on the shag-pile carpet at my youth leader's house, back propped comfortably against a familiar armchair. I had been in the youth group for two years now, and my new-found faith was growing by the day. Sat in the armchair was Gerald, a jolly man with a hefty London accent, who was talking about the Bible. Gerald loved stories – Old Testament stories especially. He loved the tales of heroes and villains, prophets and kings, rogues and heroes, which spilt across the Old Testament's pages. In those laughter-filled evenings, he taught many of us to love the stories too. Under his careful tutelage, we lost our fear of stories from such a strange time and place – and started to look to them instead for inspiration.

Another floor once again, many years later, as the tight weave of my office carpet pressed through the knees of my trousers. I found myself on my knees at the desk as I contemplated the task ahead. Yesterday I had been leading a holiday Bible club with 100 screaming children having a ball. Today, I was contemplating one of a minister's hardest tasks – the funeral of a child. Called away from the holiday club, I had stood at baby Jonah's bedside with his frightened young parents as they looked down at their precious baby. Their little boy, born with all manner of problems, would live for only forty-eight hours, and now he was gone. The church would be packed with their contemporaries – other young parents full of hope and aspiration, shaken to the core by this untimely death. Whatever could I say?

Remembering Gerald and his stories, I delved into the pages of the Old Testament, and stumbled once again upon Jonah – an ordinary man in a desperate situation. Here, surely, was a man who understood how utter hopelessness felt? Like a bugle's call over the sound of battle, his voice came to me 'In my distress, I called to the Lord and he answered me" (Jonah 2 v. 1). Forged from a contemporary story and an ancient tragedy, a sermon was born, and I quote from it below:

How did Jonah's namesake feel during the story which has just been read out? We weren't there, of course – but the writer gives us a good idea. We are told that he was 'desperate' 'lonely', 'trapped', 'distant' and 'overwhelmed'. In his own words he was "Down at the roots of the mountains with seaweed wrapped about my head"

Jonah's parents have been there...with this Jonah AND their Jonah. In the long months of waiting, in the anxious hours of delivery; in the snail's pace of ICU, with every second measured out by beeps and monitors - they have been there. Like Jonah of old - their voices have risen up out of the depths. Like Jonah of old -they have wrapped the golden thread of faith around their hearts and waited to be hoisted aloft & rescued. Like Jonah of old - their voices have NOT gone unheard and the thread of faith is still unbroken. Along with Jonah the prophet they have said "we will look again to his Holy temple'

That is a good and brave thing to do, of course, but we have to admit that sometimes God looks a whole lot further away than others. Some days he is so close that he engulfs you. Others he is little more than a small dot, a smudge on the distant horizon. On those days you know exactly what Apostle Paul meant when he wrote: "Now we see but a poor reflection as in a glass darkly, but then we shall see face to face" Until that great day comes , we stumble towards the light...sometimes tripping, sometimes falling but - always together.'

There is no need to quote the rest of the sermon here, since you can see how it was working. Old and new, prophet and parent were woven together into a single whole. That sermon, like this book, is born of the absolute conviction that the ancient stories of faith live again in the embodied reality of contemporary faith. Each both illuminates and interrogates the other. After Jonah will follow other books. We shall encounter Ruth - the Arab girl who walks blinking into the sunlight of a Jewish story. We shall met Nehemiah - a waiter turned architect whose diaries of triumph and failure still seem fresh today. These are people of faith whose stories are yours. Read on...

CHAPTER 1:
BEYOND THE NURSERY

Years ago, when my children were very small, I grew to love the characters who peopled their world. There were talking railway engines, tugboats with faces, animals who drove cars and all sorts of others. I used to think what fun it would be to go on a heavyweight TV quiz show and answer questions with great gravitas about Postman Pat or Thomas the Tank engine. The contrast between the levity of the subject and the seriousness of the task would have had a certain banal humour. To many the attempt to discuss Jonah and his whale with any degree of seriousness may seem equally implausible. After all, how can we draw any serious lessons from a story about a man swallowed by a fish? Many aspects of the story provide easy pickings for the critics. Can a man really survive such a storm? If a man were to survive it, and happened to be swallowed by a whale, is there any good reason to think that he might escape with his life? If he did survive the storm and the whale, is it reasonable to believe that he would then set about a mission which he had gone to such great pains to avoid? Not only that, but having survived storms, whale, volte-face and a dangerous mission to a hostile enemy city, are we really to believe that a 24-hour vine and a tame worm brought judgement on his head? As if the content of the story were not problem enough, there is also the fact that the story seems to have escaped the bounds of biblical scholarship and roamed off elsewhere. Yvonne Sherwood in A biblical text and its afterlives, points out that 'Jonah can regularly be spotted stomping across the pages of children's fiction'. (p.71) Surely this is little more than a religious folk tale? An honest and engaging encounter with the text will reveal that it is far more than that.

Historical setting

Over the years there has been much discussion about the dating of this curious little book. Estimates have varied from earliest dates of 800 BC to latest dates of 200 BC. Those who argue for a later date point to the specific linguistic content, saying that it shows elements of late Hebrew and Aramaic. However, Aramaic itself bears the influence of pre-Exilic Phoenician dialects, which could point to a much earlier date. Furthermore, references to the 'King of Nineveh' lean towards an age before the ascendancy of Assyria as a major power in the Ancient World. In Jonah's little tale he may well have been referred to as the 'King of Nineveh' because he was not really king of anywhere else yet! Overall, evidence seems to point to an earlier date, no later than the 6th century BC and no earlier than the 8th century BC. Archaeological remains from the period suggest that Nineveh was a walled city of about 175,000 people about 12 km in circumference. Its name, by which it is referred to in Jonah, literally means 'city of wide streets'. Like other Proverbial names such as "Paris of the orient" or "Venice of the North" it hints at the exotic whilst also betraying an ignorance of the reality. At the time of writing it would have been seen as a far distant place full of vice and iniquity about which any known details were sketchy at best.

PLACE OF WRITING

It seems reasonable to assume that Jonah was written in Israel, since it has very much the feel of a 'tract' written about the evils of the 'dirty foreigners' across the seas. The book itself says nothing about the location of its writing. Our only point of reference, as often with Old Testament stories, is the name of Jonah's father, Amittai, about whom we know nothing. However, it seems likely that it was written in the region of Lower Galilee. The writer of 2 Kings refers to Jonah as a resident of Gath Hepher (2 Kings 14 v.25) a village now known as el-Meshed, about five miles from Nazareth. The village certainly trades on its Jonah association, and houses a tomb which purports to be that of its famous prophetic son. However, there are many other place which claim a Jonah association, including Mosul in Iraq, so any real precision on this is impossible. A thorough understanding of the book and its significance will not be gained from philology, etymology or archaeology. To really understand it, we shall have to look elsewhere.

HISTORICAL INTERPRETATION

There are almost as many interpretations of Jonah as there are interpreters. To some it is a straightforward tale, and they expend much scholarship on explaining its more miraculous elements through scientific means. Others struggle with those elements whilst upholding its kernel of theological truth. Still others eschew both theology and science, and treat it purely as myth. Even amongst those who do not dismiss it as a myth, there are people willing to interpret Jonah in just about any way imaginable. In his commentary [p.70] Allen lists ten categories of literature into which it could fit, including allegory, parable, legend, novella, didactic fiction, short story and satire. Regardless of its category, imaginative interpreters have taken every element of this story and given it allegorical and theological interpretations. The hapless whale has been cast as everything from the devil swallowing the sinner, to Christ providing the prophet's means of salvation. The sailors may represent the noble pagan or the church as an instrument of God's justice. Even the worm who features later in the story, does not escape the allegorical onslaught. To some he is the devil's creature - discouraging and attacking the saints, whilst others identify him with Christ - who strips the sinner of his self-righteous protection and brings him to his senses.

Meanwhile, the man at the heart of all this has been identified by some as the archetypal sinner, and by others as a type of Christ himself - passing through storms, trials and a three day stay in his watery tomb, before emerging triumphant to conquer sin. The early church fathers certainly saw Jonah as an archetype of Christ - passing through many travails before emerging on the other side after a kind of resurrection. Centuries later, Augustine and others saw Jonah as a type of the stiff-necked and unresponsive Jew who stood opposed to Christ. When the Reformation came along, preachers like Calvin seized upon Jonah as the sloppy and unwilling disciple, who should serve as a lesson to the Christian not to behave likewise. Calvin also took great delight in the small details, reputedly noting that even the worm came at God's behest: 'the gnawing even of worms are directed by the counsel of God'. A scale of interpretation which can identify the principle character with both Christ and the sinner will prove to be a slippery slope indeed.

As if that weren't all confusing enough, Nineveh has conveniently served as a type of whichever city most attracts the opprobrium of preachers at the time. It can be anything from a den of Western iniquity to a hotbed of Eastern vice. Some years ago, when the Harry Potter sagas were new and Christians were getting themselves in a lather about whether they were moral tales or a wicked celebration of the occult, a friend of mine cut through all the discussions with his own acerbic wit. 'Harry Potter' he said, 'is the church's boggart - taking on the shape of whatever the church fears most.' (A boggart is a mythical creature in the Harry Potter tales which takes on the form of whatever people fear the most). The same could be said of Jonah's Nineveh.

In some respects it is the very simplicity of the story which makes its interpretation so diverse and complex. When my brother and I were little boys, and still young enough to be prepared, on occasion, to share a Christmas toy, someone gave us a theatre set. The whole thing was made of cardboard, and once assembled had three slots at the top. Into these you could insert your choice of backdrop, a selection of different 'wings' and finally a curtain to drop with a flourish at the end of your performance. All the characters, both individuals and groups, were supplied with a cardboard 'finger' on which they could be inserted from stage left or stage right at the critical moment. The set also included a script for your performance. However, in my recollection we were so much more interested in setting up the theatre that we soon started making up our own stories with which to animate the characters.

To examine the book of Jonah feels a bit like unpacking that play theatre from its box. As you take the characters out you set them aside one by one. Here is the cowardly Jonah with his seasick green face. There is the swarthy sea captain with his bushy beard and bulging biceps. Next comes the scary whale with his shiny skin and his little beady eyes, and the wiggly worm. Finally there is the pagan king with his plaited beard and his sandals curled up at the ends. In the box there are two backdrops too. You can choose between the grey-green sea or the crenulated walls of Nineveh. Now that it is all out of the box, you can set it up and tell the story any way you want to. Goodies and baddies can be exchanged at will, and each character can speak and act just as you choose. The characters are only two-dimensional puppets, after all, so you can tell the tale any way you want.

EXTRA BIBLICAL 'LIFE'

Of course the discussion and retelling of Jonah's story is neither restricted to the nursery nor the church. In 1891 James Bartley, a harpooner on a British Whaler, was reputedly swallowed whole by a whale. The next day, when his shipmates captured the beast, he was pulled out alive, albeit with skin and hair burnt by the acid in the whale's stomach and rendered blind. He became something of a travelling circus act before ending his days as a cobbler. His gravestone bears the legend: 'James Bartley – a modern day Jonah.'

After him there have been all manner of modern Jonahs. He has featured in poems, both epic and short, plays, artworks through the centuries, and even in George Gershwin's song 'It ain't necessarily so'. Eugene Abeshaus, a Russian Jew who emigrated to Haifa in 1976 following negotiations between Brezhnev and Carter, painted a famous image of Jonah three years later. In it a bewildered Russian Jew steps ashore in Haifa from the whale's mouth. In each hand he holds a battered suitcase, and looks around as if he doesn't quite belong. He has become a cipher for the artist's own feelings of rescue coupled with displacement and bewilderment.

It is maybe the fact Jonah can be read as comic or tragic, religious or political, that this story has found itself squeezed, remoulded and recruited to all manner of causes. At school in the early 1970s I was singing Hurd's *Jonah Man Jazz* musical without the faintest clue as to the book's theological agenda. Polish poet Zbigniew Herbert has Jonah living out his days far from Nineveh as a dealer in cattle and antiques, before dying of cancer in a 'neat hospital'. The Canadian TV series *Northern Exposure* sets one episode in the belly of Jonah's whale where the lead character has a surreal conversation with his childhood Rabbi before exiting through the rear of the whale which morphs into a New York Subway. [Sherwood p.147]

Any man who can be pressed into service by Reformation preachers, Jewish comedians, Russian painters, children's book illustrators and others has already been through the 'interpretative mill' quite enough. The purpose of this little book is not to rescue Jonah from his detractors, nor to ask that the 'real Jonah should please stand up' - for he is long gone with the passage of the years. These pages are not the place to tackle discussions about the scientific questions raised by the tale, nor to provide some authoritative conclusion to the theological debates. Instead the book aims to understand Jonah by immersion (pun fully intended). In the chapters which follow you will slink with Jonah from his family home, glancing furtively over your shoulder at what you have left behind. With him you will arrive in the unfamiliar environment of the port, wind ruffling your hair and seagull's screeches in your ears. With Jonah you will go below deck and try to outride the storm, all the time uncomfortably aware that you are to blame for the torment up above. With Jonah, you will pitch headlong into the abyss of the sea and its creature. Later, much later, you will emerge with him to face up to an unwelcome mission and its equally unwelcome outcome. You will sit and sulk with him too as he looks down on the city of Nineveh from his shelter. This is immersive theology - where truth is found in experience, and poetry is hammered out on the anvil of hardship.

To mention the word 'poetry' to some is instantly unhelpful. Their minds go back to poetry they had to learn and dissect at secondary school. Sensitive souls will remember the poem's sighing soul escaping as it underwent that kind of vivisection which we call critical analysis. The mind of others will go further back still, to the times where they were asked to write poetry of their own, and teachers would frown if it failed to rhyme. To assume that all poetry should rhyme is like thinking that all music must be classical or all art must be modern. Nothing could be further from the truth. Poetry begins with a kind of consciousness long before it becomes a means of expression.

True poetry not only attains that heightened consciousness, but knows what to do with it. The word 'poetry' originally comes from the Greek verb 'poeio' – meaning to make or fashion something. A poet attains a new understanding of his or her environment and then makes something new and exquisite out of the old materials and experiences they find to hand. This being so, sometimes the best poets are to be found in extremis, where the going is tough and the raw materials are very raw. Great poetry may often be forged of great suffering, just as the notes of blues music were originally wrung from the extreme hardship and degradation of those who wrote it. Maybe the tale of Jonah's experiences in extremis will make poets of us all.

CHAPTER 2:
THE INTERPRETATIVE BRIDGE

Some years ago I paid a visit to the gorgeous Antrim coast in Northern Ireland. It is a beautiful place, with rugged coves, crashing waves and beautiful blue waters. I had always wanted to visit the Giant's Causeway – with its bizarre 'pavement' of perfect geometric basalt pillars stretching off into the sea. It was every bit as dramatic as I had anticipated, but proved not to be the highlight of my Antrim visit. The day after my visit to the Causeway I went a little further along the coast to Carrick-a-Rede. The attraction here is the 'Fishermen's Bridge' slung between the shore and a tiny rocky island. The bridge is made from thick knotted rope, and forms a narrow 'V' down which the bravest walk. As you cross the bridge, it sways alarmingly in the sea breeze, and the waves crash and broil some twenty metres below in the narrow chasm. Though the distance between the two is not that great, it can seem like one enormous leap.

The same might be said when interpreting a book such as Jonah. After all, he inhabited a world so very different to our own. There were no cars, no computers, no speedy transportation and the understanding of the wider world was vastly different to everything we know. To look into the difference too much might bring about some of the vertigo felt at Carrick-a- Rede. The gulf seems just so deep and intimidating. Is it worth embarking upon the journey when so many things separate us? Isn't this slender volume, like its slender rope counterpart, likely to leave us feeling a little giddy in the end?

ACKNOWLEDGE THE DIFFERENCES

If we are to make the journey across the rickety bridge into Jonah's world and come back with something worth keeping, it is best to acknowledge the scale of the differences. The first and most obvious is the language. Jonah's little book was written in Hebrew, from right to left, from the back of the book to the front, in a language where vowels are only notated above and below the main text. The timbre, tone rhythm and concepts of the language are utterly alien to our own. Words which meant one thing to Jonah may well mean another thing entirely to us, even when translated. With any language there is a whole set of mental 'furniture' to which the language gives rise. This remains so even when the words themselves have been translated.

As with any language, it is only the superficial crust which conceals a bedrock of ideas beneath. The way that Jonah felt about the value of life and the likelihood of death would be strange to many of us. His view of non-Jewish foreigners would be liable to get him arrested today, and his understanding of God would seem exceptionally narrow and parochial to us. Even our concept of knowledge is different to his, influenced as it is by Greek and Roman philosophy. We tend to regard knowledge as a matter of acquiring empirical evidence. For Jonah knowledge was a relational matter – growing out of his relationship with his clan, tribe, family and ultimately his God.

His language and ideas are set against a backdrop of political and religious ferment which is outside most of our experience. Throughout the possible 'window' during which Jonah was written vast Empires were locking horns over that part of the world which we now call the Middle East. Empires were squaring up to one another, kings rose and fell, and the storms of change were raging. As the Phoenicians' star was waning, so the Babylonians and Assyrians were battling it out for ascendancy, before the Greeks changed everything. Jonah's homeland was a little dot on this ever-changing map beneath the shadow of these battling giants.

Unlike us, Jonah would have been largely unaware of the political ferment going on at his doorstep. We are accustomed to knowing all about what is happening on the other side of the world almost as soon as it has happened. Whilst our ability to assimilate such information may be limited, our capacity for acquiring it is enormous. By and large we know what is happening, where it is happening, and to whom it is happening. Places far away can seem near at hand as TV camera and the internet bring them close to us. Of course it is often said that our capacity for assimilating all this information is less than our capacity to acquire it. The 'always-on' news culture has dulled our sense of historical awareness such that we know more about what happened in the past twenty four hours than in the past twenty four years. For Jonah it would not have been so. All his information came to him by word of mouth. As such, it would have been filtered and rephrased many times before it reached his ears. His knowledge of the world beyond his village would have been limited, and his knowledge of other lands virtually non-existent.

Although a Jew by birth and religious practice, Jonah lived in an era when pagan rituals and barbaric sacrifices were little more than a generation away. We know, for instance, that the Canaanites and the Phoenicians worshipped Moloch, and their worship included a form of child sacrifice. Things which would make our blood run cold would probably have caused him to roll his eyes and mutter something about 'foreigners'. Dress him up in Western clothes, teach him to speak modern English and locate him in a house down your street – but he will still seem a world away. In all these respects he is very definitely not like us.

EMBRACE THE SIMILARITIES

Despite all of that, there are so many aspects of Jonah's story with which we can identify. These include the elemental – the raw force of nature made manifest in the crashing sea and the whale's gaping maw. Any person, of any culture or age, who has ever stared hypnotically at a raging torrent knows what this is all about. Theologians like to talk about the 'oceanic feeling' – the sense of artless wonder which we feel when confronted with creation at its most dramatic. This might be in the roaring power of a waterfall, the drama of a thunderstorm, or the drumming of hailstones on the roof overhead. The natural forces which provide the drama in Jonah's story are as familiar as the last gust of wind or the next shower of rain.

The emotional aspects of the story are familiar too. It is almost impossible that anyone should ever read Jonah's story who has not experienced the terror, anger or shame which courses through Jonah's veins. The causes may be utterly different - since few will have found themselves called to prophetic office. However, the emotions generated by the failure to do that which is most expected of us is certainly no stranger. Mothers and fathers have felt it in the home. Employers and employees have felt it in the workplace. Teachers have felt it in the classroom when they feel they are not getting their message across. Government ministers have felt it in the corridors of power, and many a minister has felt it in the church. Not only is the feeling familiar, but the selfishness which makes him resent God's decision and the doubt which makes him run are no strangers to us. We shall explore this more in subsequent chapters.

There are many social and psychological aspects to the story which seem all too familiar too. No matter how much we might care to admit it, many of us feel an unintentional unease around those who are different to us. Whether it is language, culture, creed or colour which makes them different, we find ourselves uncomfortably aware of that difference. Political correctness means that such things cannot be spoken. However, a certain frisson of unease amongst those who do not speak our language, share our experience or move to our particular rhythms is as old as humankind itself. Not only that, but Jonah's almost petulant resentment at being singled out by God is something which many have experienced. The little voice which cries within 'why me' has a very familiar ring to it.

There is something which we recognise in the supplementary characters in the story too. The pagan sailors are not one -dimensional 'cartoon baddies', but are capable of courage and nobility even in the face of adversity. Years ago a popular TV series depicted a resistance cell working in Nazi occupied Belgium during the Second World War. The Wehrmacht soldiers depicted in it came across as ordinary people in an extraordinary situation. To the amazement of both cast and screenwriters, the series *Allo Allo*, was a huge hit in Germany. It was a relief to see German soldiers from that period not depicted as entirely bad. Bad people with a good side are as familiar as the person who greets us daily in the mirror. Not only that, but a political figure who is prepared to sacrifice dignity in the interests of holding onto power is certainly recognisable. Nineveh's King would find many a sympathetic ear amongst the world's statesmen.

Through it all the theological presence of God is an unchanging thread too. The God who opened the whale's mouth is the same one who shut the mouths of Daniel's lions and put a coin in the mouth of a fish for Jesus to fetch. The God who whips up the sea into a terrible storm is the same one who, in Job's words, 'tips the water jars of heaven',(Job 38 v.37) and who will one day still the stormy sea on which Christ and his companions are travelling. Look a little deeper into the theological seams of Jonah, and you will find all manner of theological themes which run deep throughout scripture. In these pages we find a God who cares about the stranger, detests sin, and always works to change the big picture through the small intervention. All these things are the currency of faith, and we carry them around as much in our pockets as Jonah did. There is a continuity here which allows people of faith who have encountered God elsewhere in the bible's story to find him again here.

When I crossed that wobbly, swaying bridge at Carrick-a Rede I did it for three reasons. Firstly, I wanted to see the view from the island out to sea, and the view afforded of the crashing waves from the bridge itself.. Secondly, I wanted the experience. I wanted to steel my nerves and feel my heart beat a little faster. I wanted to get to the other side, take a deep breath and enjoy the feel of solid rock beneath my feet once again. Finally, I quite simply wanted to be able to say that I had done it. I wanted to be able to say that despite its danger and difficulty and downright scariness, I had conquered it and come back the richer for it.

Go on, put a foot on the rickety bridge. Venture into Jonahsland, a place inhabited by crashing seas, enormous whales, strange cities and obliging worms. Take the plunge in the pages which follow. In the end its what you bring back across the bridge which matters.

CHAPTER 3:
THE DREADED CALL

JONAH 1

Jonah Flees From the LORD

[1] The word of the LORD came to Jonah son of Amittai: [2] "Go to the great city of Nineveh and preach against it, because its wickedness has come up before me."

[3] But Jonah ran away from the LORD and headed for Tarshish. He went down to Joppa, where he found a ship bound for that port. After paying the fare, he went aboard and sailed for Tarshish to flee from the LORD.

[4] Then the LORD sent a great wind on the sea, and such a violent storm arose that the ship threatened to break up. [5] All the sailors were afraid and each cried out to his own god. And they threw the cargo into the sea to lighten the ship.

If there was a back end to the backside of the back of beyond, then this was it. Jonah's dad was somebody, or had been. 'Big in the temple' or so they said. But as for Jonah? A nobody in nowhere-town doing lots of nothing. Every day played out in the same monotone fashion. Jonah would haul himself out of bed and go about his inconsequential business leaving barely a scratch on the earth's surface. He often thought, on gazing up at the impervious sun overhead, that it's not so much as it were looking down on him – more looking through him. It looked through him as it might through a leaf skeleton – more hole than leaf, or the wings of a damsel fly – gossamer thin and lasting but a day.

He was doing just that – gazing at the unremitting sun, when The Voice came. Now had it been his father, or his father's father – they might have recognised it. Its tone might have been hidden somewhere deep in the nervous system, like a finely honed bell hanging in that inner space and waiting for the right hand to strike it. But not with him. With him it sounded strange, distant and full of dread. There was a tone somewhere on the edge of the sound that struck a chord, but the words themselves soon drove it from his consciousness. As the voice explained his mission, all the warmth of the sun drained away. First the air around turned chill, then each breath in drew its coldness down into his lungs, and finally his very veins ran thick and cold.

Jonah's horizons were small ones. He knew little of the world beyond his village; less of the town beyond that, and anything in another land might as well have been as far off as the sun high above. He had heard the word 'Nineveh' before, of course - and every syllable of its strange name filled him with dread. He had heard talk of its wickedness around the fire at night. As logs cracked and spit, so his father would spit out the accursed syllables. It was a terrible place, where men were beasts and God's good sun refused to shine. The thought that he, Jonah, might go there, charged with a mission and entrusted with a message from the world-maker himself sent him into a kind of spiritual shock. He couldn't think, couldn't pray, and even his movements seemed leaden and clumsy.

When the voice had stopped he slunk in at home, like a reveller coming home from a night of costly fun, and looked around at the few possessions which represented his ordinary life. Here was a hoe, caked with last season's mud from the field. There was a broken sandal - its thong waiting for a moment to stretch it out and thread it through the sole once again. On the floor was a stick he had been whittling and shaping these many nights - but like the carver himself it had never turned into anything much. Here, in these four walls, was a tale of shabby ordinariness writ large. Right now he would have settled for ordinary, but it was not to be. He put on his spare sandals - the tougher ones, tossed an extra travelling cloak about his shoulders, picked up the half-carved stick, threw one last glance at the room, and slipped back out again.

He had to ask two, no three times on the way about the port, but when he got near there was no mistaking it. The masts of the ships jutted up into the leaden sky, like pencil marks on a new sheet of paper. Everywhere there were sights and smells such as he had never seen. He dodged as a young boy dashed past him with a wicker basket of fresh fish, dripping briny water on his ankle as he passed. He felt it roll around the ankle bone and plummet to the sole of his sandal, squelching then with the next step. This was a strange place indeed. Instead of the dry dusts of the fields there was a salty dampness to the air. A wind fresher than he had ever felt inland ruffled his hair and tugged at the edge of his cloak. There were foreign accents and dark, swarthy faces half showing under hoods, whilst grubby children scampered between the legs of the crowds, their voices shrill and strange.

At last he stood at the quayside, staring out at the undulating monstrous sea, and wondering if it truly went on forever beyond the horizon. He'd heard tales in his childhood that the sea was full of dark and slimy creatures – untamed and vicious. If he closed his eyes he could picture them now as his grandfather had described them of old – monstrous scales like armour, evil yellow eyes and teeth like razor sharp palisades. 'Well' barked the master of the creaking vessel. 'are you coming or aren't you?' Jonah stammered his assent, handed over the only coins he had, and stepped gingerly onto the tilting wooden floor of his new home.

For the first few hours he watched as the coast slipped further and further behind. The cap of each white wave seemed to chip another piece out of the certainty he once had known. Looking out at the speckled green and grey carpet behind the boat, he wondered if he would ever be back. And if he did, would it feel like home, or would he feel like him? Already the journey had changed him, already he felt dwarfed by the secret, enormous burden God had placed on his shoulders. His only comfort was that he knew enough to run, to run away from that terrible city and God's foolish love for it. How indulgent to spoil them with a prophet, he thought. Whatever was God thinking of? The waves might rise and fall (they were doing it lots just now), kingdoms might come and go - but places like Nineveh would always be outcast and that's the way it should be. He smirked as he pictured the look on their faces when judgement eventually fell. In his hands he could feel his half-finished carving. It seemed smaller somehow out here - in the broad light of day and set against the vast ocean and the winds slapping the sails. It looked pathetic and ugly - a bit like Nineveh, no doubt. Thinking of them now and their silly foreign faces he snapped the stick in two and let the wind blow one half of it into the oblivion of the sea. The Ninevites didn't need a prophet; they needed an executioner.

His reverie was broken by the booming voice of the ship's master again. 'Get below', he shouted. 'Get below or I'll toss you overboard myself and save the waves the bother'. Jonah needed no second bidding, and his last glimpse over his shoulder as he scrambled below was a huge chest being heaved and pushed to the edge by the crew. He couldn't resist watching as it tumbled, as if in slow motion over the edge. On deck it had taken four men to move it, veins standing out on their necks and sweating to inch it along. On the boiling sea it bobbed once, twice, like a child's wooden brick, before heeling over and sinking forever out of sight.

He shuddered involuntarily and then ducked out of sight in search of a warm place to ride out the storm.

CHAPTER 4:
THE LONGEST NIGHT

JONAH 1

⁵ But Jonah had gone below deck, where he lay down and fell into a deep sleep. ⁶ The captain went to him and said, "How can you sleep? Get up and call on your god! Maybe he will take notice of us, and we will not perish."

⁷ Then the sailors said to each other, "Come, let us cast lots to find out who is responsible for this calamity." They cast lots and the lot fell on Jonah.

⁸ So they asked him, "Tell us, who is responsible for making all this trouble for us? What do you do? Where do you come from? What is your country? From what people are you?"

⁹ He answered, "I am a Hebrew and I worship the LORD, the God of heaven, who made the sea and the land."

¹⁰ This terrified them and they asked, "What have you done?" (They knew he was running away from the LORD, because he had already told them so.)

¹¹ The sea was getting rougher and rougher. So they asked him, "What should we do to you to make the sea calm down for us?"

¹² "Pick me up and throw me into the sea," he replied, "and it will become calm. I know that it is my fault that this great storm has come upon you."

¹³ Instead, the men did their best to row back to land. But they could not, for the sea grew even wilder than before. ¹⁴ Then they cried to the LORD, "O LORD, please do not let us die for taking this man's life. Do not hold us accountable for killing an innocent man, for you, O LORD, have done as you pleased." ¹⁵ Then they took Jonah and threw him overboard, and the raging sea grew calm. 16 At this the men greatly feared the LORD, and they offered a sacrifice to the LORD and made vows to him.

In Jonah's cocoon below deck he had somehow managed to muffle the sound of the storm outside. Wedged between the wooden boxes of cargo on one side and the rough earthenware jugs on the other, he had wound a loose piece of sacking round and round his weary head with its now strangely greenish complexion. Far from disturbing him, the angry sea was rocking, rocking, rocking him into a stupefied sleep. Deep down, somewhere there in the well his sleep had dug for him, there was a safe place. In it there was no sun to peer at him, no Voice to trouble him, and no evil seething city of Nineveh to await his arrival. In that little world he was heading back home, not off into the unfamiliar. Each swish of the waves was like puff of wind wafting, wafting him back home to his little room and his little life. And yet, through the fog of sleep, there was one sound which penetrated again and again through the rough wooden planks above him. It was a rattle, clunking and clattering across the deck until it came to rest. In his mind he pictured it like rough ball made of ivory, or even of metal. It obviously had sharp edges, for it thunked and banged as it rolled above his head.

It was indeed a rough thing. It had once been attached to the end of a leg bone, had sat in the leg socket of some long forgotten horse or ass. Now it was a dice, and up above on the yawing, pitching deck, it rolled to and fro. Cast from each sailor's cracked and calloused hand it tottered across the sloping wooden landscape like a drunken man trying to find his way home amongst the obstacles in his path. Occasionally it would bounce of a piece of rigging, or wedge itself against the rain-soaked flesh of a sailor's meaty leg. This was a game of dice like none they had ever known. Played out beneath the broiling, angry sky, they were playing as if their lives depended on it. Lit from time to time by the absurd flashes of lightning overhead, the crazy, ill-fashioned ball of bone would tell them who to blame for their night of terror. No-one was quite sure whether they believed in it or not. After all, every man had his own beliefs and many had their own gods. But what else were they to do? The sea was rising up like an angered spirit and somebody must surely be to blame.

Down below, Jonah settled back to sleep as the rattling overhead had ceased. With a sigh he was just pushing his furrowed brow further into the crook of his arm when the hatch overhead was flung open, admitting a rush of cold air and a cascade of seawater. Blotting out the light was the figure of the vessel's master. Before he had even opened his mouth, Jonah could feel the anger pent up in his muscular form. 'Who are you, and what have you done to anger the gods so much?' Before Jonah could think of an answer he continued. 'You come to my boat looking like some kind of stray animal that's run away from its master - and now this! I demand to know where you are from and what you have done' With each phrase his tone deepened and the volume increased until voice and thunder, thunder and voice were one single drum roll of accusation.

Jonah hung his head and explained, as he already had to some of the crew, that he was indeed a runaway. He jutted his chin out with something approaching pride, as he described himself as a Hebrew - a creature of the God who had fashioned the mountains and scraped out the bed of the sea. It struck him even as he said it that the sickly green waves, and maybe the dread creatures which swam beneath them, were the work of His hands. 'Now I have angered him', he confessed. 'I have stirred up his great heart and fired his passions and the storm reflects his anger. You must throw me in, now, without a second thought. Then perhaps you and your men can live to see another day and reach another port.'

For a moment he thought he had gone too far - offended the master's pride perhaps. The man shifted uncertainly - as if unsure whether to come down to Jonah and pick him up in his burly arms right then - or to return to the deck and slam the hatch shut on this cowardly cursed creature. In the end he did neither. Leaving Jonah below, soggy and miserable now, he returned through the open hatch to his men. Jonah strained to hear him recounting his sorry tale, then recoiled at the great boom of his voice as he ordered his men to the ship's oars. 'Pull, pull, pull' he shouted - as if trying to outshout the thunder overhead. With each shout the men would pull, the ship would clamber up the wall of the next wave, and then shudder and fall as if defeated by this backbreaking struggle. For a while Jonah watched, horribly fascinated by this enormous struggle. In the end his conscience could bear it no longer and he sought the darkness again - wedging himself between barrels and boxes - staring ahead at the rectangle of sickly yellow light in the open hatch.

Maybe his eyes had fallen shut, or maybe the lurching, bucking vessel had knocked all sense of time out of him. Either way, it seemed just moments until the rectangle was obscured by one, two, three of the sailors. They approached him as they might a rabid, cornered animal - fearing it might lash out and cause them still further harm. Jonah, however, did not. Emitting a whimper that was neither plea nor protest he yielded to their rough grasp and allowed them to manhandle him up the tilting ladder into the open air.

He took a deep breath of the salty air, and immediately retched - the feeble contents of his stomach mingling with the seawater curling round their bare and grubby feet. They looked away - not embarrassed by his sickness but theirs. These were brave men - used to wrestling the elements, accustomed to fighting the whipping, spiteful sea for their living - but quite unprepared for fighting their consciences. Gathered as if at the penitent's bench, they lined up at the side of the ship, Jonah clasped between them. Their voices rose as one in a plea whose language was strange to Jonah but whose meaning was obvious. 'Forgive us' they seemed to say, 'forgive us, mighty one for this crime against our fellow man. Forgive us for breaking the bond of humanity and the duty of hospitality. Forgive us, but we have NO CHOICE'
With the last words they hefted Jonah over the side like a barrel of unwanted cargo. As he tumbled he saw the sky - streaked with yellow and black - their faces pale with shock at what they had done, the rough planks of the ship's battered side, and then blackness.

CHAPTER 5:
THE DEEPEST PSALM

JONAH 2

Jonah's Prayer

¹ From inside the fish Jonah prayed to the Lord his God. ² He said:
"In my distress I called to the Lord, and he answered me.
From deep in the realm of the dead I called for help,
and you listened to my cry.
³ You hurled me into the depths,
into the very heart of the seas,
and the currents swirled about me;
all your waves and breakers swept over me.
⁴ I said, 'I have been banished from your sight;
yet I will look again toward your holy temple.'
⁵ The engulfing waters threatened me, the deep surrounded me;
seaweed was wrapped around my head.
⁶ To the roots of the mountains I sank down;
the earth beneath barred me in forever.
But you, Lord my God, brought my life up from the pit.
⁷ "When my life was ebbing away, I remembered you, Lord,
and my prayer rose to you, to your holy temple.
⁸ "Those who cling to worthless idols
turn away from God's love for them.
⁹ But I, with shouts of grateful praise, will sacrifice to you.
What I have vowed I will make good.
I will say, 'Salvation comes from the Lord.'"
What I have vowed I will make good.
Salvation comes from the LORD."
¹⁰ And the LORD commanded the fish, and it vomited Jonah onto dry
land.

With just an animal shriek of blind terror, half torn away by the vicious wind, the prophet, or whatever he was, was gone. The sea left no sign to mark his passing, just a clump of bubbles quickly swirled away. At once the savage wind dropped away and the huge waves died back, as if embarrassed to look on such cowardly inhumanity. A piece of torn rigging pattered, rather than slapped, on the shards of the mast. The hull, relieved to have sustained the onslaught, creaked with each rise and fall of the now gentle waves.

Awkwardly, the sailors looked each other up and down, as if they shared a guilty secret. Some looked out at the green waves, expecting to see his terrified face staring back up at them. Others looked up at the sky - wondering if whatever dwelt up there really had been appeased by such an act of treachery. Their thoughts were not good companions, and one by one they drifted away from the scene of the crime and busied themselves with mending frayed ropes and shattered timbers. The quiet, though welcome after the storm, was eerie and unnerving. The blue sky seemed false - as if someone had papered over the cracks which were there just now and made the pretence of a calm and lovely day.

Under the waters it was a different story. At first Jonah flailed and struggled - arms beating helplessly at the waters as if to claw his way back up to the surface. As the light grew dimmer, and his lungs swapped their last air for water, he sunk into an oblivion from which he would surely never escape.

So where was he now, he wondered? He opened his eyes and saw - nothing, just an impenetrable darkness in every direction. Daring to breathe at last - he filled his aching lungs and instantly regretted it. The air was foul and foetid, stinking of everything rotten in the sea and more besides. Not only that, but there was acid in the air around him too. He could feel it, pricking needle-sharp at his eyes. On the backs of his hands he felt like the hairs were burning in this fireless, cheerless place - though he couldn't see them, of course. Patting around behind him, trying to work out where he was - he realised he was sitting in a pool of gloopy, watery liquid...and beneath him the surface felt like rubber. Was this hell, he wondered? Was this the place where failed prophets came? If it were, it was no more than he deserved. Maybe it was he, rather than the wretched Ninevites, who deserved God's wrath? What was he thinking of to run from the God who stood behind, before and all about? Was there any point, he wondered, in praying down here? Could God hear him, even here? And even if he did -why ever would he answer? 'Tell me that'- he shouted. But there was no answer, nor even an echo, just a sloshing and plopping in this horrid darkness.

Old habits die hard, though - and even a failed prophet knew the psalms from the temple. Dredging deep into his memory from years gone by, in the sightless void he spoke aloud in words he'd learned from the temple, weaving, as he went the ancient with the modern...and the words of others with his own anxious cry. And right there, in the squelching darkness, a psalm was born.

CHAPTER 6:
THE RELUCTANT PREACHER

JONAH 3

Jonah Goes to Nineveh

[1] Then the word of the LORD came to Jonah a second time: [2] "Go to the great city of Nineveh and proclaim to it the message I give you."

[3] Jonah obeyed the word of the LORD and went to Nineveh. Now Nineveh was a very important city—a visit required three days. [4] On the first day, Jonah started into the city. He proclaimed: "Forty more days and Nineveh will be overturned." [5] The Ninevites believed God. They declared a fast, and all of them, from the greatest to the least, put on sackcloth.

[6] When the news reached the king of Nineveh, he rose from his throne, took off his royal robes, covered himself with sackcloth and sat down in the dust. [7] Then he issued a proclamation in Nineveh: "By the decree of the king and his nobles: Do not let any man or beast, herd or flock, taste anything; do not let them eat or drink. [8] But let man and beast be covered with sackcloth. Let everyone call urgently on God. Let them give up their evil ways and their violence. [9] Who knows? God may yet relent and with compassion turn from his fierce anger so that we will not perish."

[10] When God saw what they did and how they turned from their evil ways, he had compassion and did not bring upon them the destruction he had threatened.

Spitting the sand from his cracked lips where it had taken up unwelcome residence, Jonah pulled himself up in this strange and unwelcome place. There was the sun, again, looking down on him again. What did it see this time, he wondered? What did it see, as it baked the salt on his skin dry and began to crisp each shred of clinging seaweed until it curled and left its temporary host, wafting down to the ground? Did it see a brave man, daring to run from God? Did it see a fool - the kind of man who would seek to run from something behind him only to find it was standing in front? Or did it look through him with contempt - seeing little more than the frame of bones and shame which now held him together? Perhaps, perhaps, if he just stayed here long enough the sun would simply evaporate him away, like the seawater's splash on the jagged rocks?

He would never know, for the Voice came again. 'Jonah', it boomed. 'Jonah, go now to the great city of Nineveh and pass on the message I gave you'. Like an automaton on its little tin track, he began to walk. It was slow progress, often more falling than walking. The acid from the whale's stomach had burned his skin, and his eyes ran constantly - as if weeping for the folly which had brought him here. Times without number he would fall down, sprawling on the dusty ground and then heave himself to his feet once again. Wiping the whale tears from his eyes and the sweat from his brow he would stumble on. Moons and suns came and went without him really noticing. His stomach rumbled and his throat grew scratchy and raw. What he did eat he didn't taste and it all seemed to take him back to the hellhole of digestion in which he had been saved...or cursed...or something.

After many days the land began to rise slightly under his feet, and breaking over the horizon was the first glimpse of Nineveh, with its towering walls and frowning battlements. Already there were people about him, for the city began long before the walls. Goats nibbled at the edges of the dust road, yellow, gaunt dogs snarled and snapped as he passed by. Faces peered at him from houses and traders' stalls. As he progressed down the road, crowds began to gather. Small children would be sent scampering to cousins further down the road with tales to tell of the ragged man who was heading their way. He needed neither to hear nor understand to know what they were saying. With his burnt skin and bleached hair, with the salt clinging to the bleeding cracks on his lips, he must have looked like the walking damned. No wonder there was fear in their voices as they pointed him out to each other.

When at last he opened his mouth and begun to speak, he was amazed to find that his voice was the one thing un-weakened by his ordeal. Rather than being distorted by the stench of the ocean or scratched dry by the salt in every pore, it had a new resonance. Unlike the feeble sound of his little helpless cry in the whale's stomach it seemed to boom now. People quivered and turned their faces away as he pronounced their sentence. 'Forty days, forty days' he cried again and again like a station announcer sounding the last call for a train to nowhere. 'Forty days and it will all be over for Nineveh the great'. The more times he repeated it, the more familiar it became. It was like a child's rhyme, lulling him off into a stupor from which neither he nor these vile pagans would ever wake. They feared demise and he craved absolution with every repetition of the words.

In the end the words sprouted legs of their own. Jonah had set them running and now they clambered into every house and slithered into every brothel and scampered into every inn overturning things as they went. They respected no-one and feared no-one. Young children just learning the meaning of words, old toothless women who could barely pronounce them – all fell under their spell. Rich men told poor men about it. Wealthy women whispered it to their servants and the servants gabbled it to their husbands. Men talked about it in twos and threes on street corners – looking up at the sky as they did so, as if the clouds themselves were listening and marshalling their arsenal for destruction day. Before long the words barrelled into the King's great throne room where not even the statuesque guards with their drawn swords could stop them. On hearing them the king's face fell like a battle pennant when the wind stops and all its life is gone. Time froze for all in the room as he digested the news. Like the pattern of clouds passing over a distant mountain, the news seemed to cross his face from one side to the other. As it travelled across, so it seemed to take every last drop of sunshine and hope with it. At last he climbed slowly, deliberately down from the throne as if afraid to step in the mess he had made. Sloping away, he withdrew to his chambers and closed the vast bronze doors behind him.

When he emerged, there was a collective intake of breath. Gone was the crown, gone was the perfumed oil from hair and beard, gone were the exquisite robes. Instead he stumbled from the palace barefoot like a poor man. Tottering unevenly between the astounded guards at the palace gate he looked like a gambler who had thrown his last dice and lost everything. He sat at the courtyard's edge and stared into space from a dusty corner as his courtiers and advisers fell over each other in their rush to shed their finery and sit with the king. A long and awkward silence then ensued, for protocol forbade that anyone bar the king should break it. Self consciously, all sat in their state of unfamiliar raggedness and waited. In the end, a decision was made, and the noblemen were dispatched to the four corners of this great city – courtiers no more but messenger boys. 'A fast, a fast', they shouted. 'Let neither man nor beast eat or drink. Let mouths be used for praying, not feasting. Lift your voices and cry to the heavens that the city might live'.

Jonah picked his way through the chaos with furtive steps. He felt like a man who had lit the tinder for a hundred explosions, and now walked away, leaving them to crack and pop and flame and fizz behind his back. He had been the messenger of doom, and now its poison had spread to every single household of the city, from the poorest hovel to the palace gates. Despite himself, despite the pain in every bone and the agony of every salt encrusted cut, he smiled to himself. And somewhere as close as a whale's breath and as far as a cloud's crest a decision on Nineveh's fate was made.

CHAPTER 7:
RINGSIDE SEAT

JONAH 4

Jonah's Anger at the Lord 's Compassion
¹ But Jonah was greatly displeased and became angry. ² He prayed to the LORD, "O LORD, is this not what I said when I was still at home? That is why I was so quick to flee to Tarshish. I knew that you are a gracious and compassionate God, slow to anger and abounding in love, a God who relents from sending calamity. ³ Now, O LORD, take away my life, for it is better for me to die than to live."
⁴ But the LORD replied, "Have you any right to be angry?"
⁵ Jonah went out and sat down at a place east of the city. There he made himself a shelter, sat in its shade and waited to see what would happen to the city.

———————————

The adrenalin of his mission was ebbing now, and all Jonah's old resentment began to return, bile rising in his throat. Like a bored child, he dug and poked at the ground with the remainder of his carved stick, which had remarkably survived the ordeals with him. 'I knew it', he snarled, punctuating each word with an angry jab of the stick. 'When you kidnapped me and set me off on this ridiculous journey, I knew it wrong'. Syntax, grammar, belief and respect all began to crumble, like solid iron eaten by rust. Old certainties snapped off and wafted down to the ground - like discarded paint from the crumbling ironwork of his beliefs. He berated God for his foolish generosity, and his failure to see through the shallow repentance of Nineveh.

Despite himself, he listed all the vices he had seen on his journey through the city. He took a kind of lascivious delight in describing the gaudy prostitutes with their flapping robes and the men who sloped away from them in doorways. He warmed to his theme and went on to tell God of the grotesque wealth and the pagan temples with their many gods. It was as if he hoped to make God jealous, to make him feel affronted instead of forgiving. Failing to illicit a response, he ploughed on. By he time he got onto the nasty foods and awful smells, he was like a child uselessly pounding his fists on his father's impervious chest. 'Oh , I wish I were dead' he wailed – as if to threaten God.

The quietness and reasonable tone of God's reply when it came infuriated him more than anything. 'Have you any right to be angry?' He wanted to list all his rights, to parade them before God as a display of his anger. He wanted to start with his rights as a Jew, then to talk about his rights as a man, and end with a flourish on the rights of the prophet. He gagged on the last, and gave up the argument as lost – hoping that God would do the same.

Instead he busied himself with making a shelter. He picked a spot on a lightly wooded slope overlooking the city, and for a few blissful hours it was like being a boy again. He ranged to and fro, scouting out boughs and branches which the wind had brought down. Setting aside his precious stick, just for now, he worked like a man possessed – stacking, weaving and lodging each branch in place. Hours later, as the sun began to set, he stood back to admire his shelter. With a pang of something like homesickness, he wondered what his father might have thought of it. It had walls on three sides, , its open side facing down the hill. There was no roof, but the evening air was cool, and he was too tired to fix it now.

He picked up the half of his stick like an old friend, and took it inside the shelter. With no-one to watch, he hugged it to himself, and rocked gently to and fro. Far below, the sky turned from blue, to orange, to purple, and at last to black. Straining his eyes a little, he could pick out the shapes of Nineveh. There were the walls, soaring high to protect the broad streets from invaders. There was the king's palace to one side. And above a thousand stars, like the many eyes of God watching the scene.

CHAPTER 8:
OF WORMS & TANTRUMS

JONAH 4

Jonah's Anger at the Lord 's Compassion

⁶ Then the LORD God provided a vine and made it grow up over Jonah to give shade for his head to ease his discomfort, and Jonah was very happy about the vine. ⁷ But at dawn the next day God provided a worm, which chewed the vine so that it withered. ⁸ When the sun rose, God provided a scorching east wind, and the sun blazed on Jonah's head so that he grew faint. He wanted to die, and said, "It would be better for me to die than to live."

⁹ But God said to Jonah, "Do you have a right to be angry about the vine?"

"I do," he said. "I am angry enough to die."

¹⁰ But the LORD said, "You have been concerned about this vine, though you did not tend it or make it grow. It sprang up overnight and died overnight. ¹¹ But Nineveh has more than a hundred and twenty thousand people who cannot tell their right hand from their left, and many cattle as well. Should I not be concerned about that great city?"

Jonah woke uncomfortably, once again. Since the day he had left home he had slept in a ship, in that stinking hole, and in a dozen scrapes and hollows at the side of the road. The hot wind picked at the hairs on the back of Jonah's neck and hurled the sand at his cheek as if to grind away every bump and blemish of what...had been.He could feel it scraping, stinging, cutting even. At this rate he would be turned into one huge callous, head to toe. Already his heart had been chafed by pounding against the unremitting, granite like face of God. He shuddered to think of what had been, and hated to see what would come.

He stretched and blinked at this new unwelcome day, brushing as he did so the vine above his head. One, then two shriveled, ugly, brittle leaves fell to the unyielding earth. Looking up he could see that the vine was no more - just a twisted tangle of useless branches - much like the salted mass of unkempt hair on his unprophetic head. Standing to rail against God above or below or wherever he was, he wobbled, stumbled and fell back to earth with a little puff of dust wreathing him like exhaust fumes. Perhaps that's all they were - like the signature of a passing cart. 'A prophet once passed this way' - they seemed to say, but now there is only ...this.

Head in hands, like a child sulking at his parents, he rehearsed his litany of complaints from the previous night. 'I knew this would happen', he whinged.
'You are a gracious compassionate God" he spat, wringing every ounce of grace and compassion from his voice. 'You are slow to anger', he growled, his own anger twisting each syllable. 'You are abounding in love and relent from sending calamity' - he stumbled over calamity's four syllables, much as he had stumbled from the beach when his ghastly ordeal was spent

Pausing, as if for effect, he tried another tack, quoting the words of a greater prophet in a greater place on a greater mission...and with greater dignity.
Taking Elijah's words as his own, he puffed out his ragged chest and declared "it would be better for me to die than to live" - then sat back, savouring the silence on his hillside above the city

It was short-lived. "Angry about the vine, are we?", enquired the too familiar voice. "Angry, and then some," he replied - this wasn't over. "You have no right," God said "You didn't push its tender roots deep into the earth with your fingers. You didn't unfurl its branches. You didn't breath the breath of the grape and the sip of the wine into every tiny fibre. I did all that last night – and today its gone.'

Jonah seemed to shrink visibly as the torrent continued. "What about this city with its thousands of men and women who've lost their way? Look at them- milling about down there in their sackcloth, kicking up dust in that fragile bowl of cattle and humanity. Shouldn't I care about them?"

The silence was long...as God waited for an answer. It hung there like a balloon with no draft to pick it up and carry it to the clouds. It lingered like an awkward smell with no breeze to waft it away.

It hangs there, still.

CHAPTER 9:
ISSUES WITH
INTERPRETING JONAH

So, we have rescued Jonah from the Sunday school cupboard. We have blown away the dust accumulated through years of neglect. We have scraped away the gaudy colours of the nursery and replaced them with more gown-up hues. With a little imagination and a deep breath, we have dared to look this adult horror story full in the face. We have felt the salty slap of the sea breeze on our faces, flinched at the sharp sting of whale bile in our eyes, and watched the unravelling of a man with a mission. Slowly, agonisingly, we have seen him return from the depths of despair to the brink of success. We have seen him return to his mission and perform his duties, but with neither gladness nor conviction. Finally, we have been left wondering whether he really meant any of it.

Given all of this, it is hardly surprising that the interpretative possibilities of Jonah are so diverse. Yvonne Sherwood describes it as a 'tiny text virtually capsizing under the weight of interpretation'.[p.3] Is this so? What exactly are the weighty issues which arise from the pages of this small tale? Of course there are practically as many issues as there are interpreters to provide them. In her deeply scholarly work Dr Sherwood traces the history of Jonah's interpretation down the centuries and across the cultures. As we have seen, it has become source material for comics, playwrights, poets, jazz musicians and theologians alike. Jonah's journey has been allegorized as everything from Christ's burial and resurrection, to the exile of Jews from Germany to a new life across the Atlantic. Below I outline some of the issues which have been given particular emphasis in the narrative as I have told it.

LACK OF SELF-WORTH

To be one of God's special people was a key privilege. Even when things were at their worst, this sole fact was like a bright star in the Jewish firmament - they were chosen. From the moment when God first addressed Abraham and promised to make his descendents as numerous as 'the stars in the sky'(Genesis 22 v. 17) the die was cast. Subsequent episodes, such as the Exodus from Egypt or the giving of the Ten Commandments served only to underline this unique status. Jonah was one of these chosen people. To be not only a Jew, called and chosen, but a prophet too, was an enormous thing. To receive a prophetic calling was to find oneself ranked with some of the greatest individuals in Jewish history. For Jonah to have not only his spiritual heritage as a Jew, but the inestimable privilege of a prophetic calling, should have sent him racing to Nineveh as fast as his legs would carry him. However, as we have seen, he did the opposite. Of course we could dismiss this as mere cowardice. That would be too simple, though, surely? A cowardly man might have run away, but he would surely not have run away to sea when he had never even seen it? Furthermore, an out and out coward would certainly not have offered himself up to save the lives of others. Even a cowardly person is capable of courage, and a person who does wrong may also do right in the midst of it. Jonah may be a coward, but he is not just a coward.

Sometimes our spiritual heritage and calling serves only to underline our poor estimation of our own worth. The fact that Jonah stood in a long line of prophetic giants dwarfed him rather than encouraged him. We shall never know whether there was some underlying problem with his view of himself prior to this, since we are not privy to that information. We do know, though, that the reaction of many prophets to their calling ranged between abject terror and doubts about the wisdom of God's choice. Moses, often regarded as the first of the prophets, tried to shake off his calling with pleas of inability the moment it was given. When God broke the silence of four hundred years and called on him to lead the people out of slavery, his instant response was negative. Exodus 4 v. 10 records his response:

> Moses said to the Lord, "Pardon your servant, Lord. I have never been eloquent, neither in the past nor since you have spoken to your servant. I am slow of speech and tongue."

Jeremiah pleaded his unsuitability for the role from the outset, saying that he was not up to the job:

> "Alas, Sovereign Lord," I said, "I do not know how to speak; I am too young." (Jeremiah 1 v.6)

Isaiah was overwhelmed with his sense of unworthiness, exclaiming:

> "Woe to me! I am ruined! For I am a man of unclean lips, and I live among a people of unclean lips, and my eyes have seen the King, the Lord Almighty."

Ezekiel, meanwhile, was reduced to a gibbering wreck by his first prophetic encounter with God. All of this means that we should not, perhaps, judge Jonah too harshly if he felt overwhelmed by his call.

Furthermore, our communities of faith tend to emphasise the greatness of God and the humility of the individual. This may be underlined in many ways. Sometimes ecclesiastical architecture with its high ceilings and soaring lines is designed to accentuate the greatness of God who made all things. Architects and craftsmen have devoted centuries to achieving just that effect. Have you ever noticed that we drop our voices to a hush when entering a vast cathedral or church, even when there are no other worshippers to disturb? The nature of the space evokes such a sense of God's holiness and our relative scale that we feel we have to do it. Such ecclesiastical spaces may serve not just to accentuate the celestial grandeur of God but the earthly ordinariness of the worshipper. This effect may be further enhanced by stained-glass windows. Their depictions of characters from the Bible or saints from the annals of the church may make the ordinary worshipper feel particularly intimidated. A worshipper on a Sunday, like Jonah squinting up at the sun or glancing round at his bare little room, can feel insignificant and worse.

This can be further underlined by the hymns and songs we sing. Sometimes they are at such pains to emphasise the holiness, majesty and radiance of God, that the people singing them can feel that they are spoiling the party even by opening their mouths. My own particular church background is without a great choral tradition. The first time I ever visited a choral evensong, the Dean of the cathedral was kind enough to explain what was happening. He told me that I was not expected to 'join in' with the music, but rather to allow it to inspire me and tug me heavenwards. The experience was sublime and I shall look forward to repeating it. However, if I had been in an acutely vulnerable spiritual state, overwhelmed with my own shortcomings, it might have been a different story.

If our self-esteem is at a particularly low ebb, then even the Bible can seem to intimidate where it should be inspiring and equipping. The Bible is a great repository of stories to inspire and promises to reassure. However, those very scriptures which describe the pure, the holy and the heroic can seem to make things worse, rather than better if we are in a discouraged state to start with.. Everything about Jonah's lack of self-worth, from his furtive departure from home, to his mumbled confession to the sailors, is familiar to many. It is precisely for this reason that this little book of Jonah can be the best place to turn. Here, in its pages, we can find the sort of person we recognise. We hear ourselves in his sulks and rants. We hear the voice of God in his moments of faith too, which is precisely why a Pastor looking for a sermon at a time when God seemed far away came looking.

PREJUDICE

Jonah had never met a Ninevite - nor had his father, his grandfather nor their fathers before them. In just the same way as the Jews could be caricatured for effect as wicked bogeymen in subsequent centuries , so the Ninevites could by Jonah the Jew. The caricatures would not be based on fact – far from it. However, prejudice does not need facts, rather it thrives without them. It is prejudice which allowed the inhabitants of Dublin in the Fifteenth Century to believe that those living outside the city's palisade fence were 'beyond the pale' both physically and metaphorically. In Nazi Germany the propaganda machine stoked the flames of prejudice and ignorance by caricaturing the Jews as money grabbing schemers who should be exterminated. It fanned the flames of paranoia and ignorance for its own ends and relied on the fact that prejudice asks no questions. It is prejudice which allowed Hutu and Tutsi neighbours to hack one another to death in Rwanda despite their years of living side by side. It is prejudice which suspended neighbourliness in parts of former Yugoslavia and turned people in the same town or village against one another. We who have witnessed some of these things should not be shocked when we see Jonah terrified by the prospect of travelling to the land of the Ninevites, and disgusted by the prospect of their forgiveness. We have only to look in the mirror for confirmation that it is more than possible to harbour such dark thoughts and inclinations in the heart.

We have established in chapter 1 that Jonah was written as a corrective for the Jewish people of old. They were not to think that their elected status gave them exclusive rights to God's love and forgiveness. As the narrative of Jonah unfolds, so the gap widens between his narrow mind and God's expansive heart. This little tale, so often retold and so often 'domesticated' with children's illustrations, is a warning that a broad-hearted God will not tolerate minds and hearts which are closed to the prospect of good in our fellow man. We are reminded of this not just by Jonah's experience, but by the positive portrayals of Gentiles whom we see in this Jewish tale. The sailors on Jonah's ship are brave to the point of almost dying on his behalf. The pagan king of Nineveh responds to God's word with a speed and enthusiasm ten times that of the prophet, and his pagan subjects bend to God's will without question.

This, surely, is a tale to be read at a time when the world is more connected than it ever was, and yet our fear of the 'other' is reinforced in so many different ways. The epochal consequences of 9/11 will be discussed for many decades to come. However, one of the more obvious ones has been a deep-seated suspicion of those whose spiritual compass points to a different North. With their different scriptures and their different rituals it is all too easy to consign them to a kind of modern day Nineveh where they can do their own thing – out of sight and out of mind. Of course, that is not going to happen when the people from every place on earth live in every other place. Jonah, and his dramatic warning about the dangers of prejudice, is a timely tale indeed.

FEAR AND FOLLY

These two are inseparable bedfellows. Frightened people behave foolishly, and foolish behaviour often breeds further fears. When little Jonah in his little life was confronted by the enormity of God's vision and his prophetic calling, we should not be surprised that he was afraid. Faced with the unthinkable he did what many of us would do given the opportunity – ran as fast and as far as he could in the opposite direction! In so doing he brought shame upon his family, danger to the sailors on their boat, a potentially catastrophic delay to the people of Nineveh, and disappointment to the God who had called him. As is often the case, one foolish act necessitates another to cover it up, and then another and another. As that particular snowball of folly hurtles downhill it gathers momentum and catches other people up into it. Jonah's private moment of panic became a very public thing once it started to involve people outside his village, his country and his faith. As the final chapter of Jonah reminds us, the lives of "ten thousand people and many cattle too" (Jonah 4 v11) were caught up in this tale.

Many years ago, when serious illness afflicted my family, one of the first pieces of advice I was given was this: don't make any big decisions whilst under this kind of stress. The trouble with stress is that it is a silent and insidious thief of sanity. Decisions made whilst you feel you are coping perfectly well with your stress can embarrass the one who makes them and affect the lives of those around them. If Jonah could have watched his flight from God, his foolish voyage his reluctant preaching and his petulant argument with God from a position of detached calm, he would have been mortified. The trouble is, he could not. Stress is all but invisible to the person experiencing it, which is what makes it so dangerous.

Jonah comes as a cautionary tale to any of us who find ourselves acting entirely out of character. If I am normally a person of prayer, and find myself incapable of praying - what is the matter? If I am usually willing to embrace different people and accept different points of view but find myself dismissing them out of hand - what is going on inside? If I have an equable spirit and a gentle manner but find myself lashing out in an uncontrolled way - is something more fundamental upsetting my equilibrium? Jonah's foolish behaviour, born of his fear to obey God, is a mirror held up to all people of faith. Do I recognise the way the person in that mirror is behaving - and if not, am I afraid of something?

IRRESPONSIBILITY

Peter Pan might not seem like the most obvious companion for Jonah and his whale, but there is a connection. People in and beyond the Baby Boomer generation did not grow up with the hardships which had faced their parents. They no longer had to take the burden of maturity at the kind of early age which had been required of those growing up in wartime. This in turn can lead to a Peter Pan-esque rejection of growing up. As people wait longer and longer to 'settle down' (however that may be interpreted) they live instead through a kind of extended adolescence, where pleasing yourself in both career and leisure choices is the key imperative. One of the consequences of growing up is that we gradually learn to be less selfish. A baby is the epicentre of their own universe, crying when they don't get the comfort or attention that they need in order to survive. As the baby becomes a toddler, they begin to learn the difficult lesson that they exist in a world of competing needs, where theirs may not be the first or only desire to be met. Adolescents no longer expect other people to meet their every need, but they do resent their needs being thwarted by the needs or preferences of others. When we talk about an 'extended adolescence' we imply that a primarily selfish worldview is continued into what we normally call adult life.

Jonah comes as a corrective to just such an attitude. In his story we see the drastic and irrefutable consequences of one man's selfish actions. His rejection of his prophetic calling is not a private religious dispute between a man and his God. This is not like Elijah's argument with God where he collapses from mental and physical exhaustion after his showdown on Mount Carmel. When he collapses, exhausted, on the slopes of Mount Horeb in 1 Kings 19, at least his job is already done. On that occasion only he and God are witness to his sulks and self-pity. The same could not be said for Jonah. His behaviour ends up affecting a crew of sailors, a King, a populous city, and for that matter a whale, a gourd and a worm! His actions and his reluctance are not a personal matter at all.

This is a message we really need to hear in a day when many choose to insulate their lives from others. Advances in technology mean that we can connect with others across the world in ways which were impossible one generation ago. News feeds and information can be delivered from one side of the world to the other in hundredths of a second. However, this self-same technology can also develop a kind of 'silo' mentality – where we monitor the needs of close friends and distant situations from the privacy of our own home without ever truly engaging with them. It is perfectly possible to know twice as much about the needs of others and do half as much about it as people did in generations gone by. Jonah reminds that privatised faith is not God's kind of faith at all.

DUTY

Duty is an unpopular and old-fashioned word. We tend to associate it with doing things you don't really mean but which you feel you ought to. The duty of an Old Testament prophet was to express the mind and heart of God in the clearest and most unequivocal fashion possible. Their duty started and ended with the calling. Anything beyond it was frippery, and anything less than it was cowardice. Men like Ezekiel learnt about the cost of their prophetic duty when it cost him the life of the woman he loved. (Ezekiel 24 v. 15 - 17) Jeremiah learnt about the cost of duty when he could only fulfil his duty to God by angering his king. Alone in his dungeon scrolls snipped up and burnt by the king, Jeremiah's prophetic duty was nonetheless intact. (Jeremiah 38) Today it is a sense of duty which keeps a soldier going whilst under fire or a doctor answering a crash call in the small hours of the night. Duty allows us to transcend personal preference with a sense of serving some higher aim.

Ironically in Jonah, the finest examples of duty are seen elsewhere than in the prophet himself. When the storm first starts to batter Jonah's escape boat, a duty of hospitality dictates that his life must be preserved at all costs. As the storm grows worse and the waves grow higher the sailors are driven by the law of the sea which pits man against his arch enemy and declares that the life of a passenger is sacrosanct. Only at the last minute do they cave in and abandon their duty of care. As the story unfolds, the whale does what is expected of it, as does the gourd and the worm. At the other end of the scale, the King of Nineveh behaves as duty expects him to - protecting the lives of his subjects from harm. His swift response to Jonah's preaching spares the lives of those who look to him for protection and governance.

Jonah's little tale stands as a reminder of the cost when God's people shirk their duty. Had he been successful in his attempt to run away, then Nineveh, together with its thousands of inhabitants, would surely have perished. As Edmund Burke once said, 'all that is necessary for evil to triumph is for good men to do nothing'. In many of the upheavals going on around the world it is the politically, rather than the spiritually motivated who have the upper hand. A re-reading of Jonah can serve as a pick-me-up to the weary soul – reminding us that God may require any one of us to speak or act on his behalf for the sake of those whom we have never met and whose needs we have never considered.

RESENTMENT & SCHADENFREUDE

Schadenfreude is one of those German words which never quite translates into English. Literally it means "joy over shame' and describes that glee which we feel when we see someone else getting what is coming to them. Tabloid newspapers rely on it – damning the self-same people on their front pages whose downfall they have engineered. Broadsheets do it as well, albeit in a slightly more subtle way. Sometimes they can be responsible for building the very podiums from which the mighty are toppled, and then laughing and pointing as they roll on the ground.

Of course, to a certain extent we do that with Jonah. From our privileged vantage point as readers we can see him as the cowardly and small-hearted individual that he is. We tut disapprovingly when he runs away to Tarshish. We roll our eyes when the poor sailors nearly drown trying to save him. We nod knowingly when the whale swallows him up and he prays penitently from its belly. When he stumbles reluctantly onto the beach we shake our heads as if this was bound to happen all along and if we were in his position we would have just got right on and done it without all the fuss.

When the final scene is played out, though, we go very quiet. We all know that he is being small minded and selfish-hearted wanting to see Nineveh's destruction – but we had rather hoped to see it too. Anyone who has ever laughed at the downfall of a famous person, or jeered a talent show contestant off the television knows what Jonah chapter 4 is all about. Reflected in those pages we see a certain impish delight in the misfortune of others which would drive us all if we allowed it to do so.

Maybe Sherwood is right that this little tale is "virtually capsizing under the weight of interpretation". However, the more I read it the more I become convinced that we are the ones capsizing, rather than the tale itself. Jonah rolls up underneath our cosy little boat like an unruly wave on the sea - tipping us out and obliging us to flail around until we find our way again. This, surely, is why the tale has never grown old?

Chapter 10:
Shaking Hands With Jonah

Writing in his commentary on Jonah in 1980, Leslie Allen wrote that 'a Jonah lurks in every Christian heart'. Whilst this is undoubtedly true, I believe we are dealing with not one, but several Jonahs here. We are all capable of being different kinds of Jonah at different points in our lives.

Home Jonah

This Jonah is perfectly happy with his ordinary (and anonymous) life, thank you very much. We find him in his own home, surrounded by his creature comforts and not in the least inclined to go anywhere else. The fates of those far away across the seas may be a real concern, but they are not his real concern. God's arrival on the doorstep of his heart and mind are no more welcome than being door-stepped by someone who is trying to sell us tea towels or a new electricity supplier. We didn't ask for it and we don't want it. Jonah is not alone in this. Jeremiah, arguably one of the noblest of the Old Testament prophets, was so surprised when God came calling that he wondered whether he had got the right man. Ezekiel, a temporary resident in a canal side refugee camp, was reduced to a whimpering wreck when his moment of call came. Even the great Moses was so astounded at God's call that he tried to dodge it, and ended up passing the spokesman's role onto his brother.

There are doubtless numerous reasons for this kind of reaction. On occasions it might be sheer laziness. Like Homer Simpson on his beloved sofa we are comfortably settled and we really don't want to move. It can be a mental laziness too – we simply don't want to stretch our minds and imaginations as far as those who live beyond the horizon. When people first began to coin the phrase 'compassion fatigue' it was exactly this to which they were referring. Sometimes there is a more sinister driver too. The comfort and security of our home depends on our sense of being protected from the world outside. Years ago designer Roger Dean designed a house with a built in sound system to amplify the sounds of the world outside. On a windy day it would amplify the sound of the wind howling outside and when the rain beat down it would heighten the sound of it lashing against the windows. In this way, the comfort of the people inside would be heightened precisely by their sense of being kept away from what was going on outside. In a similar way, we sometimes like to heighten our sense of security by keeping the world and its needs as firmly shut outside the door as we possibly can. Home Jonah's home is definitely his castle, and visitors are not welcome.

HARBOUR JONAH

This Jonah has stopped feeling resentful or sullen about God's intrusion on his home, and has decided to do something about it. He can no longer feel comfortable at home, so he has decided to leave it. He has left for the the nearest port, and found himself a nice ship heading away from Nineveh and its unwelcome call upon him. Upset and afraid by God's calling, he has decided to put as much distance between God and himself as he possibly can.

I've met this Jonah on many occasions, though rarely in church. Sometimes he's running away from an awkward and unpleasant encounter with God in his childhood. Other times, his fingers were burnt in a church where he was asked to do too much and given too little support. There's plenty of energy there, and usually lots of compassion. Like Jonah, though, its been turned in a new direction. Like Jonah pounding down to the docks as fast as his legs would carry him, this man has broken a sweat over new, different and definitely non-religious projects. It would be a mistake to see him as irreligious. If anything, he is post- religious, since he has tasted something of religion and has turned away to leave it behind.

If any of us ever happen to meet Harbour Jonah, it is worth reflecting on the range of emotions he is experiencing. Fear is undoubtedly a factor, but there are other things at work too. Resentment runs deep in this man's veins. His carefully ordered life has been irreparably upset by God's intervention. If Jonah were pushing a proverbial apple cart at the start of the story, apples all stacked in neat rows – then by the end he is chasing them in all directions. That's just the point though – he is chasing them. Harbour Jonah may be heading in the wrong direction, but he is heading somewhere. This is a resourceful man, and he deserves some credit for that.

HOLD JONAH

This Jonah has had his spat with God, he's run away from home, he's installed himself on the ship, and now he's letting others do the work. Whilst up top the world is being rent apart by a storm and others fight to save their skin and his, he slumbers peacefully down in the hold. He doesn't mean to put them in danger, but then again he's not overly bothered about them either. What he doesn't realise is that his private fight with God isn't private any more. Others are being drawn in, as if on the edges of a whirlpool, and the damage is spreading.

Sometimes I've met this Jonah in Christian ministry. He or she has been so wounded in God's service that they begin to 'shut down' as a means of self-protection. Like Jonah in the hold, they shut themselves away and do the barest minimum, confident that no-one will notice. We often joke about ministers 'only working Sundays – but a bruised minster can end up doing just that. Hurting and dejected, they restrict themselves to 'keeping the show going' on their one public appearance of the week. Their hope is that so long as Sunday services take place, no-one will notice if other things are neglected. They do notice, though, that's the problem. The church or organisation for which they work begins to pitch and toss and crack apart at the seams. All this is because the person who should have a sense of spiritual responsibility has abandoned it, and many suffer the consequences. Clearly it is outwith the capacity of this little book to address such an issue. However, it needs to be noted that attrition in Christian ministry is a tragedy both for the ministers and the church. Hold Jonah was a prophet who cam within a whisker of drowning. How many others come as close to sinking, I wonder?

DECK JONAH

This Jonah to be found up on deck and he is truly magnificent. Having realised that his actions have put the lives of others in danger, he rises to the occasion and offers his own life for their safety. This is no dramatic gesture – he really means it and is prepared to go through with it. We can only imagine how the minutes or hours must have stretched out between his first offer, and the time when the sailors felt that they had no alternative but to accept it. Flash in the pan bravery is one thing, but standing by your costly word in the storm is quite another. This is not bravado, either. Instead, the prophet has woken up to his genuine responsibility for the situation and has offered to pay the highest price to put it right.

This is not a Jonah we often meet. We live in a culture where many have honed their skills of guilt displacement to the nth degree. Often we will blame the government, or the teachers, or the churches, or even God himself before we dream of looking in the mirror for the culprit. Sometimes the storm can only be stilled if the key person owns up to their faults – even if that key person is me.

For some, the most important reason to revisit the pages of this ancient tale is in order to encounter Deck Jonah, and to find his moment of courage for themselves. A secret long shared, a guilt long festering, a relationship long neglected might all find a ray of hope in his courageous voice raised above the wind and the waves.

CITY JONAH

I'm tempted to call this one smelly Jonah, since that is undoubtedly what he would have been on his unseemly exit from the whale's stomach. However, that is hardly fair, for the point here is that he is at last getting on with the very thing to which God called him at the outset of the story. Not only that, but it takes some grit and determination to do it. Expecting people to take you seriously when you squelch into their city smelling of whale bile takes some doing, or some chutzpah as Jonah himself might have called it. When we take into account that this personal preaching tour took three whole days, we realise that it was quite some undertaking. Back and forth across the streets and alleys of that great city he treks, until the message reaches even the King himself. Having bowed to the inevitable, Jonah gets on with the job.

This Jonah is to be found in many a Seminary and Missionary Training College. Occasionally you can find him in a language school too. Convinced, sometimes after a long battle, that God has a job for him to do; he puts his head down and sees it through. This Jonah combines conviction with determination and a fair sprinkling of stubbornness too. Nothing, but nothing will delay or deflect him until the task is complete.

If you have committed yourself to a task for which the preparation seems interminable, then this is definitely the Jonah for you. For many, the preparatory stages for mission or ministry seem to go on and on. The excitement and thrill which they felt when acknowledging a call seem to get lost in the long hours of lectures, or the endless learning of vocabulary in a strange tongue. What seemed like a call to the glamorous or the exotic now seems as humdrum as preparing new paintwork for redecoration – it just goes on and on. To spend some time with City Jonah, as he criss-crosses the city on his long mission, might be just the inspiration you need.

HILL JONAH

Oh dear! This Jonah may have done his job and seen it through to the bitter end, but on the hill we discover that he didn't really mean it. Throughout his three day preaching tour of Nineveh - it seems as if he did it from the head but definitely not from the heart. All along there was a growing sense of dread and a gathering cloud of anger at God's inclination to forgive those whom he would rather destroy. Up here on the hill he sinks into a trough of despond and gloom. Whilst we know about God's attempts to dislodge him from it with a vine, a worm and a jolly good talking to - we have no idea whether it was successful. Our last glimpse of Jonah is of him sitting on the hillside amidst the wreckage of his bower, fuming at his creator and rescuer.

This may just be the Jonah that Leslie Allen was describing, for he is undoubtedly the most common. Whatever convictions he once had, and no matter what brave things he has undertaken for God in the past, there is a problem now. He disagrees with God's set of priorities and resents the generosity of his heart. He and God are barely on speaking terms, though he stays in church just to spite him.

Jonah may be an ancient book, and he may have travelled by ancient boat to a city now reduced to rubble in the desert sands, but the issues he raises are uncomfortably contemporary. I was brought face to face with this when discussing the story with a man who teaches English to asylum seekers. They are often dismissed as unwanted, unwelcome and worthy only of contempt. Reading Jonah's words in a contemporary translation he commented that he sounded 'just like a tabloid journalist'! Indeed he does, with their rants about leaving 'them to their fate' and their insistence that 'charity begins at home' Jonah would doubtless have fitted right in amongst their ranks.

Many scholars believe that Jonah was written as a 'tract' to correct the narrow and exclusive mindset of the Jewish people. They were so convinced of their special status in God's created order that they could not possibly conceive of him wishing to forgive anybody else. Such was the extent of this conviction that many might have been tempted to cheer Jonah on in his flight to Tarshish and to sulk alongside him in his bower on the hillside. Of course they would never have openly condoned anyone disobeying God, but even so like Jonah we find ourselves caught between our prejudices and God's grace. We sense that there is a clash between our common sense and God's uncommon mercy.

Jonah also brings us face to face with the consequences of our failure to do things God's way. Even though we might sympathise with his misgivings, we cannot really condone this cowardly little man as he runs away, puts other lives in danger and then pouts like a spoilt child. The story, surely, makes us aware that a failure to abide by God's guidance is not a purely private affair? His behaviour endangered the lives of the sailors, and would have led the Ninevites to an untimely end had God not intervened directly.

A Jonah may 'lurk in every heart', but its when we let him out into words and actions that he really runs amok. Perhaps he should be dealt with in the heart before he goes any further.

If Jonah is indeed a poet in extremis, we maybe need to find a way back to God in *our* extremis. As we have noted, a poet is a person who makes new reality out of the old realities he finds lying about him. Like a skilled metal worker he puts this with that and twists things around in the heat as the sparks fly and something new is forged. Poetry is a work of re-creation, where the old is made new whilst retaining the essence of the old. It is maybe only through our immersion in this old tale of bitterness, cowardice and failure that something new can emerge. One of the highest aspirations of faith, surely, is that a faith marinated in all the bittersweet experiences of life still comes out tasting rich and full of the presence of God?

Using what you have read, and the study notes which follow, I urge you to plunge into Jonah's experience in extremis, and allow God to forge something new on the anvil of the soul. This is not only poetry, but theology, in extremis.

STUDY NOTES

These notes may be used by individuals or groups, to help you reflect on Jonah's experience...and maybe even to create some poetry in extremis!

Chapter 3: The Dreaded Call

This chapter deals with the surprising nature of God's call, and his curious logic in the people he chooses

- Many of the Bible's leading characters seem to struggle to believe that God would want to make use of them. Gideon is incredulous, Jeremiah is shocked, and Moses goes so far as to question God's sincerity. Why might this be?
- If you had to list the qualities of a spokesperson for God, what would they be?
- How would you describe Jonah's mood in this chapter?
- The Bible is silent on Jonah's reasons for running away - but what do you think they might have been?
- If you met him on the road to Tarshish, what would you say to him to try and dissuade him from running away?

This episode provides a valuable catalyst to reflect on those moments in our own lives when God's call appears to us to be misplaced, exaggerated, or downright impossible. Are there moments when you have felt equally convicted both of God's call and your ability to fulfil it? Whilst some say that God equips the called, rather than calling the equipped, it can still feel like a tough ask.

Instead of dwelling on those things which every Christian is called to do - like praying and sharing what they have with others, think about those things which are specific to you. A call may comprise natural gifts, accumulated experience, shaped character, and supernatural confirmations - which may be anything from verses of scripture to prophetic words. Is God calling you to do something particular? If so, acknowledge the call in prayer, ask others to pray with you, and start to investigate how you might pursue it further.

CHAPTER 4: THE LONGEST NIGHT

This chapter really is Jonah's dark night of the soul - made worse by the fact that it is of his own making. It provides an opportunity for us to reflect on where God is to be found in the darkest moments. Often it is in the most unexpected places.

- Can you think of times when you found yourself in a crisis of your own making?
- If other people, like the sailors were being brave around you - did that make you feel better or worse?
- How do you think Jonah's original readers would have felt about the behaviour of the sailors?
- Is the storm symbolic of God's anger, or is He just trying to turn Jonah around?

Sometimes when the storm is raging, we lack either energy or headspace to reflect on what God is doing and saying. Chapters like this allow us to learn from someone else's experience and then store the lessons away ready for when it is our turn. This chapter in particular allows us to see that when we and others are caught up in the storm, evidence of real human goodness may not be far away.

If you can, spend some time reflecting on a troubled time through which you have passed. Where was God to be found in it? Did you find him in the comforting words of Scripture, as many do? Perhaps you found him in the uplifting words of fellow Christians. It may even be that you found Him in the words and actions of those who do not share your faith.

Jonah never got to thank those who did their best to save him. Is there someone you need to thank today?

CHAPTER 5: THE DEEPEST PSALM

This chapter contains one of the most poignant and heartfelt pieces of poetry in the entire Bible. If you are studying it in a group, it might be worthwhile allowing everybody the opportunity to read it aloud. In this way, you can hear the pathos reflected in different voices.

- 'You hurled, your waves. your breakers' make it sound as if this is God's personal assault upon Jonah. Is it?
- Do times of hardship make you more, or less inclined to pray?
- Jonah's language in the Psalm appears to echo the phrases we find elsewhere in the Old Testament. Is there such a thing as a vocabulary of faith, do you think?
- There seems to be a change of tempo, or at least of mood part way through the Psalm. Where would you say it is to be found?

It seems as if Jonah had to sink, literally, as far as he could go before he had the inclination to look up. After a catalogue of misfortune which started with his rebellion, his faith begins to turn a corner as the words "I will" creep into his vocabulary. Maybe there is always one of these turning points in the moment of faith's crisis.

Take a little time to compose your own 'blue' Psalm, reflecting on how and where you have found God in your moments of crisis. If you are doing this in a group setting, there may only be one or two who can do it. Others may wish to take what they have heard and compose something of their own at home.

CHAPTER 6: THE RELUCTANT PREACHER

The fact that Jonah survives his ordeal at all is remarkable. However, the gusto with which he preaches and the effect it has on the entire population of the enormous city of Nineveh is astonishing. This chapter gives us pause to reflect on the power of the preached word, and its effect for good and ill. It also demonstrates that the word may have a power quite independent of those who preach it.

- If you saw Jonah walking towards you - skin bleached, eyebrows burnt and clothes ragged - would you listen to his message?
- How do you account for the rapid and powerful response to Jonah's message?
- Which travels faster - good news or bad?
- If you were in Jonah's position, how would you be feeling at the end of this chapter?

Jonah was bruised, battered, smelly and altogether disreputable. Few Christians would have invited him to preach in their churches - or at least not without taking a good shower first! Sometimes it seems as if the message really is more powerful than the messenger.

This would be a good moment to pause and pray for all those who communicate God's message. Some do it in pulpits, some in the streets, and some through the mass media of television and radio. Pray that they might be encouraged as they see fruit from their work.

CHAPTER 7: RINGSIDE SEAT

There can be no doubt that in this chapter we see Jonah behaving very badly indeed. In his heart he harboured a desire for the destruction of Nineveh's people, and in his words he allowed his anger with God to take a hold. Although they are expressed here in an extreme form, the chances are that we recognise both the key emotions Jonah displays here.

- If you had to explain what Jonah was feeling and why to a person unfamiliar with the story, what would you say?
- When Jonah talks about wishing that he had never left home, does he remind you of other voices in the Old Testament?
- Are there times when we find God's forgiveness hard to accept or understand? If so, what might they be?
- What answer to do you think God expected to his question in v.4?
- If Jonah had made room for you beside him in his shelter as the sun went down over Nineveh, what would you have said to him?

As with most of the 'biographical' books in the Bible, Jonah functions as something of mirror - reflecting our own emotions and concerns back to us. There are times when we have all felt reluctant to forgive, and would rather close our hearts than open them.

Read through this chapter again on your own, and then find a quiet place where you can talk to God. Now would be a good moment to tell God about the people or situations which you find hard to forgive.

CHAPTER 8: OF WORMS AND TANTRUMS

For Jonah, this encounter is the final straw. It proves to be for us, too, as we never know its outcome. In the end the theological and philosophical arguments about sin, grace and forgiveness all come down to a vine, a worm and an unanswered question.

- Why exactly is Jonah so angry?
- Since Jonah has (reluctantly) done his job and delivered his message - why is this whole episode with the worm and the vine necessary?
- The writer of the story leaves us in the dark as to whether or not it has a happy ending with Jonah changing his mind. What do you think?
- Write a letter to Jonah on behalf of the City Council of Nineveh.

This chapter suggests that God is interested in more than just 'getting the job done'. In the end he wants to change not just the fate of Nineveh and its people, but the internal climate within Jonah's heart. The message may have been delivered and the crisis averted, but the story is definitely not over.

There are many areas in all our lives where our hearts are smaller than God's. At times we are acutely aware that we forgive more reluctantly than him and forget less effectively than him. In general we have more problems remembering things we should forget than forgetting things we should remember. If God chooses to forgive and forget the sin of another, then so should we. Take a little time to thank God that he always forgives the sinner - not least you!

THE EXTRA CHAPTER

Many years ago, when it was still 'pc' to do such things, the Cub Scouts used to do a bob-a-job week. Even after decimalisation, it still went by the same name. Cub Scouts would go round the neighbourhood offering to do practical tasks such as shopping, gardening, car cleaning and other simple jobs. Once the job was done, then money was paid to Cub Scout funds, and a yellow "job done" sticker was handed over. The bright yellow sticker featured a big tick and the words "job done". When stuck in the window it prevented the householder from being pestered by any more well-meaning Cubs.

I sometimes feel that by the end of Jonah Chapter 3, the writer should have stuck a big yellow 'job done' sticker on the page and been done with it:

✓	Prophet called
✓	Prophet reprimanded
✓	Prophet rescued and delivered
✓	Sermon preached
✓	People repented
✓	City rescued

So why the extra chapter?

When we read at the end of Jonah Chapter 3 that God 'did not bring upon them the destruction he had threatened', it feels like a real 'happy ever after' moment. The Ninevites' sin has been spotted from on high, God has summoned a prophet (albeit a reluctant one) to their city, he has preached a dire message of repentance, and they have duly repented. If we were watching a film of the story, this is the point at which the cameras would pull back to a gorgeous sunset over the City of Nineveh and the titles would roll.

Clearly, though, that is not how God sees it. Although the people have been saved, there is still at least one soul full of darkness and hatred. As long as that soul remains, the story is not over. Despite the fact that the Ninevites have repented and disaster has been averted, God seems discontent to leave it at that as long as his prophet is unconvinced by the wisdom of his actions. It is as if Jonah's dark thoughts and selfish nature are the flies in God's forgiving ointment, and they just have to be removed.

The reasons for this are not entirely clear. God seems to pay very little attention to how Isaiah feels about the people to whom he preaches, for instance. Jeremiah rants and raves about his woes as a prophet, but God never feels obliged to set him straight. God's job is to inspire, the prophet's job is to preach and that is that. Or is it?

Very often the prophet must engage personally with the message he delivers - sometimes at great cost. Hosea is told to go and marry someone who will be unfaithful to him. (Hosea 1 v.2) He will give his heart to her in marriage, she will break it when she leaves him, and he will be a laughing stock to all who hear of it. Only in this way can he feel the disappointment and betrayal which God feels from his people. Similarly, when Ezekiel's wife dies,(Ezekiel 24) he is expected to treat it as an object lesson of God's judgement on the people. When people regard Jeremiah as the most sublime of the prophets, it is probably because he comes so close to sharing God's own agony over the fate of his people. At times the verbal and physical suffering of prophet who speaks and God who inspires seem so intertwined that it is hard to tell one from the other.

If this is the case, then Jonah reluctantly 'handing the goods over' would never be enough, would it? Nineveh's rescue is only half the story, so long as there is a prophet with a calloused heart sitting on the hill. Far from being an unexpected add-on, Chapter 4 is the conclusion without which the story would be incomplete. Jonah, as God's man, must not only do God's bidding but sense God's longing.

Many years ago I caught a few sentences of a radio talk by a Jewish Rabbi. I had only just got into the car and missed most of what he had to say. The Rabbi was discussing the Exodus story, and the moment when the army pursuing the Israelites was drowned as the Red Sea closed over them. I only heard the last sentence or two, but the gist of what the Rabbi was saying was that God was aggrieved at the sight- since the Egyptians were in some sense his children too. I have struggled and struggled to find any reference to this ever again...until now.

Last night I wrote to a Jewish friend in Amsterdam, asking whether there was any possibility she could track down this half-remembered story. Providentially she had a Jewish scholar staying with her at the time, and the two of them mined this gem out of a Talmudic commentary on the Jewish Scriptures for me. In Talmud Megilla 10b we read the following, just after Pharaoh and his army have drowned and the angels want to celebrate.

The ministering angels wanted to chant their hymns, but the Holy One, blessed be He, said : the works of my hands is being drowned in the sea, and shall you chant hymns?'

The subsequent Rabbinical interpretations of this seem to range to and fro, with some embracing it wholly, and others trying to find any which way for God *not* to call the Egyptians the work of his hands. However, a God who can send Jonah all that way (twice) and send a worm to rain on his parade to make him think about the fate of the Ninevites seems more than capable of hushing the angels as they rejoice over the destruction of the Egyptian army.

If this really is axiomatic to God's character, then Chapter 4 becomes far more than a codicil at the end of Jonah's story. It is not so much that chapter 4 is added as an afterthought - more that chapters 1 - 3 are inserted as a prelude. If the book is really more about the fate of the

Jews than it is the fate of the Ninevites, then this sordid little scene with a fat worm, a munched vine, and a sulky prophet is its climax. Like the cameos in Amos chapter 1 and 2, the rest of Jonah has led the initial readers right up the garden path, to the point where they are more than ready to sit with Jonah, arms folded, brow furrowed and a look of petulant anger on their faces. Why should God behave like that?

Why should he indeed? Chapter 4's true brilliance is that the question is never answered. Nineveh's salvation is clear. Jonah's discomfort is clear. God's decision is clear. Only one of those three things could change – and it won't be God's mind or Nineveh's fate.

This is the fourth book I have written, and the first in this series of Biblical characters brought to life. Normally I linger long and hard over how to finish them. Often a book can be the product of two, three or more years' work. Along the way there have been writes, re-writes, scrumpled sheets, research, requests for permission to quote and whole host of checks and edits. When it comes to choosing the last sentence of the book there is a slight sense of awe. It feels like bringing down the curtain on a grand production, writing the final note for an orchestral masterpiece, or dabbing the final speck of colour onto a work of art. How to finish what has gone before?

The writer of Jonah's little tale is untroubled by this. He finds a device more striking than the brightest blob of paint and more resonant than the mellowest note. His finishing touch is...a question mark. By that one sole device he catapults the book across the centuries and into the laps...and hearts of all who will read it. Finishing on such a note, we cannot be anything but troubled by the story's conclusion. What did Jonah say? What did Jonah do? And for that matter – what would we have said or done?

Inspired by my eloquent forebear, perhaps I should finish this book in the same way?

BIBLIOGRAPHY

Leslie Allen, *The New International Commentary on the Old Testament: The books of Joel, Obadiah, Jonah and Micah* (Eerdmans , Grand Rapids. 1980)

David W Baker, T. Desmond Alexander & Bruce Waltke, *Tyndale Old Testament Commentary on Obadiah, Jonah and Micah* (IVP, Leicester, 1988)

Ellen Dannin, *Yom Kippur: On Jonah and more - getting perspective in order to repent* (Jewish Reconstructionist Federation, October 2007)

M.R de Haan, *Jonah: Fact or Fiction* (Zondervan. Grand Rapids, 1982)

Philip Jensen, *Reading Jonah* (Grove, Cambridge, 1999)

R.T. Kendall, *Jonah: An Exposition* (Paternoster, Carlisle, 1995)

James Robinson, *Jonah's Scrapbook Journal* (Durham, 2010)

Yvonne Sherwood, *A Biblical Text and its Afterlives: The Survival of Jonah in Western Culture* (Cambridge University Press, Cambridge, 2001)

Acknowledgements

Cover illustration is by Jonny Gallant

'The Jonah Cycle' illustration is by Natalia Luptova

'Jonah's big fish' illustration is by James Robinson

Quotes from Yvonne Sherwood are by kind permission of Cambridge University Press.